On Politics
and the Art
of
Acting

BY ARTHUR MILLER

DRAMA

The Golden Years · The Man Who Had All the Luck
All My Sons · Death of a Salesman
An Enemy of the People (*adaptation of the play by Ibsen*)
The Crucible · A View from the Bridge · After the Fall
Incident at Vichy · The Price · The American Clock
The Creation of the World and Other Business
The Archbishop's Ceiling · The Ride Down Mt. Morgan
Broken Glass · Mr. Peters' Connections

ONE-ACT PLAYS

A View from the Bridge, *one-act version, with* A Memory of Two Mondays
Elegy for a Lady (*in* Two-Way Mirror)
Some Kind of Love Story (*in* Two-Way Mirror)
I Can't Remember Anything (*in* Danger: Memory!)
Clara (*in* Danger: Memory!) · The Last Yankee

OTHER WORKS

Situation Normal · The Misfits (*a cinema novel*)
Focus (*a novel*) · I Don't Need You Anymore (*short stories*)
In the Country (*reportage with Inge Morath photographs*)
Chinese Encounters (*reportage with Inge Morath photographs*)
In Russia (*reportage with Inge Morath photographs*)
Salesman in Beijing (*a memoir*) · Timebends (*autobiography*)
Homely Girl, A Life (*novella*)

COLLECTIONS

Arthur Miller's Collected Plays (Volumes I and II)
The Portable Arthur Miller
The Theater Essays of Arthur Miller (*Robert Martin, editor*)
Echoes Down the Corridor: Collected Essays, 1944–2000
(*Stephen R. Centola, editor*)

TELEVISION WORKS
Playing for Time

SCREENPLAYS
The Misfits · Everybody Wins · The Crucible

ARTHUR MILLER

On Politics
and the Art
of
Acting

VIKING

VIKING

Published by the Penguin Group
Penguin Putnam Inc., 375 Hudson Street,
New York, New York 10014, U.S.A.
Penguin Books Ltd, 27 Wrights Lane, London W8 5TZ, England
Penguin Books Australia Ltd, Ringwood, Victoria, Australia
Penguin Books Canada Ltd, 10 Alcorn Avenue,
Toronto, Ontario, Canada M4V 3B2
Penguin Books (N.Z.) Ltd, 182-190 Wairau Road,
Auckland 10, New Zealand

Penguin Books Ltd, Registered Offices:
Harmondsworth, Middlesex, England

First published in 2001 by Viking Penguin,
a member of Penguin Putnam Inc.

1   3   5   7   9   10   8   6   4   2

This work first appeared in different form in *Harper's Magazine.*

ISBN 0-670-03042-2
CIP data available.

This book is printed on acid-free paper. ∞

Printed in the United States of America
Set in Centaur
Designed by Francesca Belanger

*H*ere are some observations about politicians as actors. Since some of my best friends are actors, I don't dare say anything bad about the art itself. The fact is that acting is inevitable as soon as we walk out our front doors and into society. I am acting now; certainly I am not speaking in the same tone as I would in my living room. It is not news that we are moved more by our glandular reactions to a leader's personality, his acting, than by his proposals or by his moral character. To their millions of followers, after all, many of them highly intelligent university intellectuals, Hitler and Stalin were profoundly moral men, revealers of new truths. It is true that dictators arise out of collapsing societies, so that the license to dominate is handed to them and it is not merely their talent as performers that gives them power. But something similar can be said about actors lucky enough to appear in plays or films whose time has come, rather than in old worn-out stories or those too novel for the public to grasp. Aristotle thought man was by nature a social animal, and in fact we are ruled more by the arts of performance—by acting, in other words—than anybody wants to think about for very long.

The mystery of the leader-as-performer is as ancient as civilization but in our time television has created a quantitative change in its nature; one of the oddest things about millions of lives now is that ordinary individuals, as never before in human history, are so surrounded—one might say, besieged—by acting. Twenty-four hours a day everything seen on the tube is either acted or conducted by actors in the shape of news anchormen and -women, including their hairdos. It may be that the most impressionable form of experience now for many if not most people consists of their emotional transactions with actors, which happen far more of the time than with real people. For years now commentators have had lots of fun with Reagan's inability to distinguish movies he had seen from actual events in which he had participated, but in this as in so much else he was representative of a common perplexity when a person's experience so often comes at him through the acting art. In other periods, a person might have confronted the arts of performance once a year in a church ceremony or in a rare appearance by a costumed prince or king and his ritualistic gestures; it would have seemed very strange that ordinary folk would be so subjected every day to the persuasions of professionals whose studied technique, after all, was to assume the character of someone who was not them.

Is this persistent experience of any importance? I can't imagine how to prove this, but it seems to me that when one is surrounded by such a roiling mass of consciously contrived performances it gets harder and harder for a lot of people to locate reality anymore. Admittedly, we live in an age of entertainment, but is it a good thing that our political life, for one, be so profoundly governed by the modes of theater, from tragedy to vaudeville to farce? I find myself speculating whether the relentless daily diet of crafted, acted emotions and canned ideas is not subtly pressing our brains not only to mistake fantasy for what is real but also to absorb this process into our personal sensory mechanism. This last election is an example. Obviously we must get on with life, but apparently we are now called upon to act as though nothing very unusual happened and as though nothing in our democratic ways has deteriorated, as for instance our claim to the right to instruct lesser countries on how to conduct fair elections. So, in a subtle way, we are induced to become actors, too. The show, after all,

Thumbs

must go on, even if the audience is now obliged to join in the acting. Needless to add that we shall continue instructing others on how they ought to count votes, but is our monitory voice not thinned somewhat as others hear it, and a cynicism reinforced as to our claims to being the model democracy? Or perhaps not. Perhaps very little can be expected to be retained in memory before the battering of our minds by the flotsam flowing at us on the information river.

Political leaders everywhere have come to understand that to govern they must learn how to act. No differently than any actor, Al Gore apparently rummaged through several changes of costume before finding the right mix to express the personality he thought it profitable to project. Up to the campaign he seemed an essentially serious man with no great claim to merry humor, but the presidential-type character he felt he had to play was apparently happy, upbeat, with a kind of Bing Crosby mellowness. I daresay that if he seemed so awkward it was partly because the adopted image was not really his, he had cast himself in a role that was wrong for him, as not infrequently happens to unlucky actors cast in films and theater. The original production of *Death of a Salesman*, for example, veered very close to disaster because the director and I were trying to be too faithful to a stage direction I had written into the script describing Willy as a small man. We proceeded to audition every small actor we could find, some very good ones among them, but the role in their hands seemed to be diminished into a kind of complaint, far from what was intended. In fact, there was a heroic aspect to the part which a Lee Cobb—over six feet tall and weighing nearly two hundred pounds—could effortlessly bring out, at least in rehearsal. Of course once an audience takes its seats these effects are extremely difficult to predict. I think this is so because, fundamentally, a play is trying to create an individual out of a mob, a single unified reaction out of a thousand individual ones whose interactions are mysterious. The political leader faces the same task and uncertainty, neither more nor less. Whether calculatedly or instinctively, he has to find the magnetic core that will draw together a fragmented public, and is thus obliged to try to avoid sending signals that might alienate significant sectors of his audience. Inevitably, this kind of management of an audience requires acting.

The difficult question of sincerity, therefore, arises from the very nature of persuasion itself, and with it, inevitably, the question of lying or shaving the edges of inconvenient truths. Hence, the resort to acting, to performing a role. I would like to believe—and often do—that most American congressmen and senators most of the time are probably saying in public what they also say in private, if only because consistency costs them little when they have few listeners anyway and little to lose. But the burning white light focused on the American presidential candidate is of a very different order when his election may mean a new direction for the country and a threat or reassurance to business and government in many other parts of the world. Thus the television lens becomes a microscope with the world at the eyepiece. Now the candidate's self-control, his steadiness under fire, is dangerously magnified and becomes as crucial to his success as it is to the actor facing a thousand critics as he stands alone in a spotlight surrounded by darkness on a stage.

Power, of course, changes how people act, and George W. Bush, now that he is president, seems to have learned not to sneer quite so much, and to cease furtively glancing left and right when leading up to a punch line, followed by a sharp nod to flash that he has successfully delivered it. This is bad acting, because all this dire overemphasis casts doubt on the

text. Obviously, as the sparkly magic veil of actual power has descended upon him, he has become more relaxed and confident, like an actor after he has read some hit reviews and knows the show is in for a run.

At this point I suppose I should add something about my own bias toward acting and actors. I recall the day, back in the fifties, during Eisenhower's campaign against Adlai Stevenson, when I turned on my television and saw the general who had led the greatest invasion force in history lying back under the hands of a professional makeup woman preparing him for his TV appearance. I was far more naive then, and so I still found it hard to believe that henceforth we were to be wooed and won by rouge, lipstick, and powder rather than ideas and positions on public issues. It was almost as though he were getting ready to go on in the role of General Eisenhower instead of simply *being* him. In politics, of course, what you see is rarely what you get, but in fact

Eisenhower was not a good actor, especially when he ad-libbed, disserving himself as a nearly comical bumbler with the English language when in fact he was actually a lot more literate and sophisticated than his fumbling public-speaking style suggested. As his biographer, a *Life* editor named Emmet John Hughes, once told me, Eisenhower, when he was still a junior officer, was the author of all those smoothly euphonious, rather Roman-style speeches that had made his boss, Douglas MacArthur, seem on the verge of donning a toga. Then again, I wonder if Eisenhower's syntactical stumbling in public made him seem more convincingly sincere.

Watching some of our leaders on TV has made me wonder if we really have any idea what is involved in the actor's art, and I recall again a story once told me by my old friend the late Robert Lewis, director of a number of beautiful Broadway productions, including the original *Brigadoon*. Starting out as an

Candor as discomfort

actor in the late twenties, Bobby had been the assis-
tant and dresser of Jacob Ben-Ami, a star in Europe
and in New York as well. Ben-Ami, an extraordinary
actor, was in a Yiddish play, but despite the language
and the location of the theater far from Times
Square, on the Lower East Side of Manhattan, one
of its scenes had turned it into a substantial hit with
English-speaking audiences. Experiencing that scene
had become the in thing to do in New York. People
who had never dreamed of seeing a Yiddish play trav-
eled downtown to watch this one scene, and then left.
In it Ben-Ami stood at the edge of the stage staring
into space and, with tremendous tension, brought a
revolver to his head. Seconds passed, whole minutes.
Some in the audience shut their eyes or turned away,
certain the shot was coming at any instant. Ben-Ami
clenched his jaws. Sweat broke out on his face. His
eyes seemed about to pop out of his head; his hands
trembled as he strove to will himself to suicide. More

17

moments passed. People in the audience were gasping for breath and making strange asphyxiated noises. Finally, standing on his toes now as though to leap into the unknown, Ben-Ami dropped the gun and cried out, *"Ikh ken nit!"* I can't do it! Night after night he brought the house down; Ben-Ami somehow compelled the audience to suspend its disbelief and to imagine his brains splattered all over the stage.

Lewis, aspiring young actor that he was, begged Ben-Ami to tell him the secret of how he had created this emotional reality, but the actor kept putting him off, saying he would tell him only after the final performance. "It's better for people not to know," he said, "or it'll spoil the show."

Then at last the final performance came, and at its end Ben-Ami sat in his dressing room with the young Lewis.

"You promised to tell me," Lewis said.

"All right. I'll tell you. My problem with this scene," Ben-Ami explained, "was that I personally could never blow my brains out. I am just not suicidal, and I can't imagine ending my life. So I could never really know how that man was feeling, and I could never play such a person authentically. For weeks I went around trying to think of some parallel in my own life that I could draw on. What situation could I be in where, first of all, I am standing up, I am alone, I am looking straight ahead, and something I feel I must do is making me absolutely terrified, and finally that whatever it is I can't do it?"

"Yes," Lewis said, hungry for this great actor's key to greatness. "And what is that?"

"Well," Ben-Ami said, "I finally realized that the one thing I hate worse than anything is washing in cold water. So what I'm really doing with that gun to my head is, I'm trying to get myself to step into an ice-cold shower."

Now, if we transfer this situation to political campaigns, who are we really voting for: the self-possessed character who projects dignity, exemplary morals and forthright courage enough to lead us in war or depression, or is he simply good at characterizing a counterfeit with the help of professional coaching, executive tailoring, and that array of technological pretense which the grooming of the president can now employ? Are we allowed anymore to know what is going on not in the candidate's facial expression and his choice of suit but in his head? Unfortunately, as with Ben-Ami, this is something we are not told until he is securely in office and his auditioning ends. During the campaign, for example, Mr. Bush made much of his interest in supporting education, child-protective measures, as well as the environmental protections, but within days of his administration's accession he moved to weaken one environmental protection after another, his budget shortchanged education and slashed the budget of child-protection agencies. After spending tens of millions of dollars, both candidates—at least for me—never managed to create that unmistakable click of recognition as to who they really were and it may well be that at least in Mr. Bush's case he knew the agenda he really had in mind would lose him votes, if revealed too soon and this very possibly was why one had so much trouble locating him as a real individual. As for Gore, it is impossible to know how true to his programs he would have turned out to be, but his surprising announcement of support during the campaign for the Florida Cubans in their refusal to turn over Elián González to the boy's father may well have signaled a more general opportunism; we will never know. In any case, that the Cubans' votes would ever go to a Democrat was so unlikely that the gesture toward them seemed inept even as politics, especially when for many of his followers it put Gore's integrity in question.

But stepping back from all this one has to wonder if it is simply silly to expect consistency or even coherence in candidates for national office when they are obliged to placate interests that in fact are in direct conflict with one another.

The so-called Stanislavsky system came into vogue at the dawn of the twentieth century, when science was recognized as the dominating force of the age. Objective scientific analysis promised to open everything to human control, and the Stanislavsky method was an attempt to systematize the actor's vagrant search for authenticity as he works to portray a character different from his own. Politicians do something similar all the time; by assuming personalities not genuinely theirs—let's say six-pack, lunchbox types—they hope to connect with ordinary Americans. The difficulty for Bush and Gore in their attempts to seem like regular fellas was that both were scions of successful and powerful families.

Simple, straight and truthful

Worse yet for their regular-fella personae, both were in effect created by the culture of Washington, D.C., but since you can't hope to be president without running against Washington they had to run against themselves, something which surely did not add reality to either of them. The problem for Gore was that Washington meant Clinton, whom he dared not acknowledge lest he be challenged on moral grounds. As for Bush, he was forced to impersonate an outsider pitching against dependency on the federal government, whose payroll, however, had helped feed two generations of his family. There's a name for this sort of cannonading of Washington; it is called acting. To some important degree both gentlemen had to act themselves out of their real personae into freshly begotten ones. The reality, of course, was that the closest thing on the political stage to a man of the people was Clinton the Unclean, the real goods with the six-pack background, whom it was both dangerous and necessary to disown. This took a monstrous amount of acting.

Perhaps it needs to be said that as a general rule, an axiom if you will, the closer one approaches any kind of power the more acting is required. The question is: How much? Masks and makeup go back to primitive times, of course. Men transform how they look and talk in order to draw down powers upon themselves which their ordinary behavior cannot possess. Classical Greek plays were originally performed by actors on low stilts and probably speaking through megaphones concealed inside masks, this in order to appear superhuman, godlike and in contact with obscure, transformative forces of nature and life itself. Our judges wear robes to remind us of their impersonal, objective powers of just discernment and the sanctity of the long tradition behind them. Police are uniformed as proof of their powers to control certain behavior in others; I once happened to pass a New

York bar during the Saint Patrick's Day parade and saw half a dozen cops rolling out of it with open cans of beer in their fists, their uniform jackets hanging wide showing their pistols, their caps tipped back on their heads. The small shock I felt came out of a certain ingrained respect for that uniform, which means power of a sort and ought not be worn by a drunk, and one with a pistol on his hip besides. But we are so accustomed to power signals that we rarely notice them, and so they are difficult to track in our consciousness. Yet democracy's future depends, needless to say, on how well we recognize and control them.

Roosevelt is said to have feared only one politician as a contender for the presidency against him, and that was Huey Long of Louisiana. Long, the subject of Robert Penn Warren's novel *All the King's Men*, was a demagogue, a flimflam artist railing against the corporations and castigating the rich while milking them for enormous donations, at the same time building a university and hospital system even as he used his state police to terrorize opponents, some of whom he probably had ordered murdered. Had he not been assassinated he might well have, as many feared, reached the highest levels of national power. His rise was no doubt the most impressive victory of sheer acting ability this country has ever known. Long, in his particular way, had a brilliant understanding of the performance art, the actor's ability to manufacture love and caring for his audience while emptying their pockets. More than once over these last decades I have found myself recalling one of his passing remarks, "When Fascism comes to America it will be called anti-Fascism"; he understood that many a passionate anti-Hitler politician was racist and for sale to the highest bidder. As few others, Huey Long had as much of a grasp of power's ability to create illusion in the service to his cause as a willingness to use it.

Huey Long imitating himself

In the recent campaign it was in the so-called debates that the feeling of a contrived performance came to a head, in contrast to the naked clash of personalities and ideas one had been led to expect. Here was acting, acting with a vengeance. But the consensus seems to have called the performances decidedly boring. And how could it be otherwise when both men seemed to be attempting to display the same genial temperament, competing with a readiness to perform the same role and trying, in effect, to slip into the identical gray suit for a quiet Sunday row around the lake? The role, of course, was that of the nice guy, the mildness was all Bing Crosby with a sprinkling of Bob Hope. Clearly they had both been coached not to threaten the audience with too much passion, but rather to reassure that if elected they would not disturb any reasonable person's sleep. In acting terms there was no inner reality, no genuineness, no glimpse into their unruly souls. One remarkable thing did happen, though—a single, split-second shot that revealed Gore shaking his head in helpless disbelief at some inanity Bush had spoken. Significantly, this brief display earned him many bad press reviews for what were called his superior airs, his sneering disrespect; in short, he had stepped out of costume and revealed his reality. The American press is made up of disguised theater critics; substance counts for next to nothing compared with style and inventive characterization. The question is whether the guy is persuasive, not what he is persuading us of. For a millisecond Gore's style had collapsed and he had been inept enough to have gotten real! And this clown wanted to be *president* yet! Not only is all the world a stage, but we seem at times to have all but obliterated the fine line between the feigned and the real.

To an old memory like mine it all seems so engineered, so bereft of a kind of rousing celebratory joy that one used to connect with the craziness of

American political campaigning. Our latter-day candidates are like insurance salesmen at a picnic, morticians at a burlesque show, they simply can't drop their dreary preoccupations with their professional poses and join in the fun. When the boredom becomes painful I recall a speech Roosevelt gave in, I believe, Boston during one of his four campaigns. The Republican congressional leaders at the time were a man named Fish, another Joe Martin and a third was Barton. These were the bane of his existence, blocking everything he was trying to accomplish in Washington. Before the Boston crowd now he would put forward a proposal and then ask why it had not been enacted. The answer, "Martin, Barton and Fish!" Then he would cite another proposal and once again ask who had stopped it dead—"Martin, Barton and Fish!" Now the rhythm caught on and he rode it like a galloping horse, putting out one thwarted proposal after another followed by the massive crowd's howling with laughter and roaring back the response "Martin, Barton and Fish!" Where have all the happy guys gone with their razzing ironies? Or is it that the country is so sourly defensive now that the fundamental absurdity of it all is intolerable to contemplate anymore?

In that speech Roosevelt was manifestly performing, unifying a crowd with a rhythmic repetition. But the substance—his thwarted program—never got lost in his and the crowd's enjoyment. Indeed, reality was even better defined by his satire, the border kept intact between it and fantasy.

Was there ever a border? It is hard to know, but we might try to visualize the Lincoln-Douglas debates before the Civil War, when thousands would stand, spread out across some pasture, to listen to the two speakers, who were mounted on stumps so they could be seen from far off. There certainly was no makeup; neither man had a speechwriter but, incredibly enough, made it all up himself. In fact, years later Lincoln wrote the final version of the Gettysburg Address on scraps of paper on his way to a memorial meeting. Is it imaginable that any of our candidates could have such conviction and, more importantly, such self-assured candor as to move him to pour out his heart this way? To be sure, Lincoln and Douglas, at least in the record of their remarks, were civil to each other, but the attack on each other's ideas was sharp and thorough, revealing of their actual approaches to the nation's problems. As for their styles, they had to have been very different than the current laid-back cool before the lens. The lens magnifies everything: one slight lift of an eyelid and you look like you're glaring. If there is a single, most basic requirement for success on television it is minimalization: before the camera, whatever you are doing, do less of it and emit cool. In other words—act. In contrast, speakers facing hundreds of people without a microphone and in the open air must inevitably have been broader in gesture and even more emphatic in speech than in life. Likewise, their use of language had to be more pointed and precise in order to carry their points out to the edges of the crowd. And no makeup artist stood waiting to wipe up every bead of sweat on a speaker's lip; the candidates were stripped to their shirtsleeves in the summer heat, and people nearby could no doubt smell them. There may, in short, have been some aspect of human reality in such a debate.

I had one memorable lesson in the camera's tendency to exaggerate movement when, on the last day of shooting *The Misfits,* I watched Clark Gable in the final shot of the picture. Sitting behind the wheel of his truck he watched as Marilyn, some yards ahead, unbound his dog's leash from a stake in the ground. The camera rolled and I waited for the spread of happiness across his face; he was supposed to cast a look of intense warmth and love toward her as she worked offscreen, but watching from beside the camera a dozen feet away from him I could see no change in his expression. "Cut!" I turned to John Huston who, apparently satisfied, was going over to shake Gable's hand at the completion of this final shot of the film.

Next day I saw the shot on the screen. A look of profound happiness was spread across Gable's face, and his eyes were lit up with joy. I confessed to Gable, sitting beside me in the screening room, that I was sure he'd done nothing. He framed his eyes with both hands; "Movie acting is all up here," he said, indicating his eyes, "and the less the better."

But for political debaters, shying away from the camera's exaggerating tendency may in itself have a dampening effect on their spontaneity and willingness to engage in conflict. There were times in this last campaign when one even wondered whether the candidates feared that to really raise issues and engage in a genuine clash before the camera might dangerously set fire to some of the more flammable public. But of course there is a veritable plague of benign smiling on the glass screen, quite as if a revealing scowl or passionate outburst might ignite some kind of social conflagration.

No differently than with actors, the single most important characteristic a politician needs to display is relaxed sincerity. Thinking back to the great stars of the past it is hard to recall one of them who did not have a certain underlying cool, a self-assurance that suggests the heroic. Bogart or Stewart, Edward G. Robinson or Cagney, Widmark or Wayne or Mitchum, whatever they were in private, as leading men they seemed unconflicted and at home with themselves. Ronald Reagan disarmed his opponents by never showing the slightest sign of inner conflict about the truth of what he was saying. Simple-

minded as his critics found his ideas and remarks, cyn-
ical and manipulative as he may have been in actuality, he seemed to believe every word he said.
He could tell you that atmospheric pollution came
from trees, or that ketchup was a vegetable in school
lunches, or leave the impression that he had seen
action in World War II rather than in a movie he had
made or perhaps only seen, and if you didn't believe
these things you were still kind of amused by how
sincerely he said them. Sincerity implies honesty, an
absence of moral conflict in the mind of its posses-
sor. Of course, this can also indicate insensitivity or
even stupidity. It is hard, for example, to think of
another American official whose reputation would
not have been stained by saluting a cemetery of Nazi
dead with heartfelt solemnity while barely mention-
ing the many millions of victims of their vile regime,
including Americans. But Reagan was not only an
actor; he loved acting and it can be said that at least

in public he not only acted all the time but did so sincerely. The second best actor is Clinton, who does occasionally seem to blush, but then again he was caught in an illicit sexual act, which is far more important than illegally shipping restricted weapons to foreign countries. Reagan's tendency to confuse events in films with things that really happened is often seen as intellectual weakness, but in reality it was—unknowingly, of course—a Stanislavskian triumph, the very consummation of the actor's ability to incorporate reality into the fantasy of his role. In Reagan the dividing line between acting and actuality was simply melted, gone. And what we want from leading men is quite the same thing as we demand of our leaders, the reassurance that we are in the hands of one who has mastered events and his own uncertainties. Human beings, as the poet said, cannot bear very much reality, and the art of politics is our best proof. The trouble is that a leader somehow comes to

Love ya

symbolize his country, and so the nagging question is whether, when real trouble comes, we can act ourselves out of it.

The parallels between acting and politics are really innumerable and, depending on your point of view, as discouraging as they are inevitable. The first obligation of the actor, for example, just as with a politician, is to get himself known. P. T. Barnum said it for all time when a reporter asked if he wasn't ashamed at having tricked the public. He had originated the freak show, which had drawn an immense audience to his Bridgeport, Connecticut, barn to see the bearded lady and the two-headed calf. But the show was such a great hit that his problem was how to get people to leave and make room for new customers. His solution was to put up a sign, with an arrow pointing to the door that read, "This way to the Egress." Since nobody had ever seen an "egress" before, the place emptied satisfactorily, and the audience found itself in the street. The reporter asked if this ploy wouldn't anger people and ruin his reputation. Barnum gave his historic reply: "I don't care what they write about me as long as they spell my name right." If there is a single rubric to express the most basic requirement for political or theatrical success, this is it.

Whether he admits it or not, the actor wants not only to be believed and admired but to be loved, and what may help to account for the dullness of this last campaign was the absence of affection for either man, not to speak of love. By the end it seemed like an unpopularity contest, a competition for who was less disliked by more people than the other, a demonstration of negative consent. Put another way, in theatrical terms these were character actors but not fascinating stars. Ironically, the exception to all this lovelessness was Nader, whose people, at least on television, did seem to adore their leader, even after he had managed to help wreck Gore and elect Bush, whom they certainly despised far more than they did Gore, whose technical defeat they ended up helping to seal. We are so accustomed to thinking of politicians as hardheaded, but as with certain movies and plays the whole enterprise threatens to turn into illusion, an incoherent dream.

It occurs to me at this point that I ought to confess that I have known only one president whom I feel confident about calling "the President of the United States," and that was Franklin Roosevelt. My impulse is to say that he alone was not an actor, but I probably think that because he was such a good one. He could not stand on his legs, after all, but he took care never to exhibit weakness by appearing in his wheelchair, or in any mood but that of upbeat, cheery optimism, which at times he most certainly did not feel. Roosevelt was so genuine a star, his presence so overwhelming, that Republicans, consciously or not, have never stopped running against him for this whole half century.

For me the Roosevelt phenomenon is both heartening and mystifying. Heartening because he was an example of a conservative, upper-class gentle-man—he initially campaigned as a strict budget balancer who was able to open himself to the dreadful realities of ordinary American life of the time, changing his whole vision of the role of government in order to relieve the suffering he had initially seemed inured to. In the process he also caused a profound change in how Americans viewed themselves, and I am probably as good an example of this shift as any.

My maternal grandfather, his finances flattened by the 1929 stock market crash, had moved into my family home. He had been a businessman all his life and a Republican. An awakening teenager, I contracted from him a profound respect for President

Herbert Hoover, with whose pained efforts I sympathized as he sought some solution to the intensifying crisis which every week seemed to sink the economy lower than anyone had thought possible. In my grandfather's view This Roosevelt—"This" was like his first name in our house—was a disgrace to humanity for presuming to challenge a suffering chief executive who was doing everything possible to help the country out of the swamp. I can clearly remember my outrage at the sight of Roosevelt's pictures in the papers, and his cold, haughty challenges to Hoover's floundering.

Roosevelt got elected and for the first famous hundred days of his administration turned the government upside down, launching new agencies to vigorously tackle the crisis of unemployment, the dispossession of the middle class, the real hunger that was so widespread across the country. The days of Denial had given way to Acknowledgment and we were all awakened as from a doze, given license to recognize the wreckage of a failed system. My old vision of Roosevelt fell to pieces and a new one arose out of the shards, that of brave truth teller, big-hearted and rather joyous welcomer of the new. The very process of revising my sense of Roosevelt from negative to positive probably affected my own way of thinking about the world. The change, however, was based not upon the new president's way with words but on his approach to issues that directly affected me and my family. We had arrived at a point where eviction from our home was a real possibility and a frightening one for a hard-working, thoroughly bourgeois nest. Nor were we alone; there were thousands of quiet streets with six-room houses like ours whose occupants were getting little sleep at night as the unimaginable was becoming quite likely. Then, as though from heaven, arrived the new Home Owners Loan Corporation, a Roosevelt innovation which

The star

simply stretched our mortgage from twenty to forty years, so that the monthly payment due was not the hundred dollars or more that it had been, but twenty-five. Along with most Americans we found no difficulty in blessing the president of the United States with whom a bond was formed that lasted until his death. The Depression really lasted a decade, far longer for nonwhites, and one learned to expect some necessary help from government which further deepened one's connection to FDR, who seemed to at least be trying to grapple with realities. One loved the statement of Harry Hopkins, his closest lieutenant, who early on had replied to the Republican attempt to placate the country by repeating that "in the long run" the economy would straighten itself out. "People," Hopkins said, "do not eat in the long run, they eat every day." In college I had a fifteen-dollar-a-month job paid for by the National Youth Administration, without which I would have had to leave school. And after graduation, I joined the Federal Theatre for its last six months of life, at twenty-two dollars and seventy-seven cents a week, during which time I wrote a tragedy and began to write commercial radio plays, work which would support me for the next six or seven years until I wrote *All My Sons.* But the point of all this is somewhat different than the obvious.

As the years passed, I found myself at odds with Roosevelt's policies on various issues, particularly his having joined the British in enforcing the spuriously named nonintervention policy toward the Spanish Civil War. Brought on by General Franco's Nazi- and Mussolini-supported rebellion, the war sparked the worldwide outrage of intellectuals and labor who saw Franco as the epitome of reaction and his victory a harbinger of worse to come. Like the British government, the Americans had embargoed the Republic even as the German and Italian Fascists were pouring in troops and planes for the Franco side. It was said that under nonintervention the Republic, desperate for arms and supplies, was forbidden to draw on some sixty million desperately needed dollars in gold deposited in New York banks. American support of a Republic in Spain might well have tipped the balance as it would have left a democracy standing intact on Hitler's flank instead of a cooperating Fascist regime for which the nonintervention policy had no doubt helped clear the way. For many, myself included, this policy raised a grave question mark on Roosevelt's liberalism.

In later years I would read, in the autobiography of Harold Ickes, Roosevelt's secretary of the Interior and perhaps the most relentlessly honest politician I have ever heard of, that through the four years of the Spanish Civil War, Ickes had tried at the weekly Cabinet meetings to get the president to reconsider his Spanish policy, but Ickes was never allowed time or opportunity to speak to the issue. One day, soon after the war had ended with Franco in Madrid, Roosevelt was being helped out of the Cabinet meeting room when he stopped his chair and beckoned Ickes to him. Ickes came and bent over and Roosevelt said that Spain was the greatest mistake he had ever made.

For many, probably most of my generation, the willful paralysis of the democracies toward Fascism's takeover of the legitimately elected Spanish government was the guarantee of a second world war if only because it would demoralize anti-Fascism in the rest of Europe and embolden Hitler. If there was one man who could have made the difference it was Roosevelt, and he had turned his back. And he had done the same with the pleas of a shipload of Jewish refugees, men, women and children who had arrived from Germany on the *St. Louis,* and were denied entry into America and had to return to Nazi Germany and their fate.

These were terribly serious failings in a leader claiming a commitment to the democratic ethos. Some were saying he had supported the Spanish Fascists for fear of losing the Catholic vote in his coming reelection bid. As for the tragic *St. Louis* incident, he was seen as having chosen not to confront American anti-Semitism should he order the six hundred passengers admitted rather than sent back to their deaths. There were some very good reasons to reevaluate one's belief in Roosevelt. There were days when it seemed he had fooled a lot of people who had trusted in him.

And yet, even as I began to see cynicism where I would earlier have denied it, and the ugly face of political advantage where principle should have ruled, it was all but impossible to dismiss him as another charlatan. To this day I can't see a photo of him without feeling something like pride and a certain happiness which I seem to take in his style. It is emphatically not that I have carefully compared his positive and negative points, but something far less rational that keeps him a noble figure for me. Objectively, I am sure, the good he did far outweighs the evil, but no verdict based on reason ought to so utterly blot out his bad deeds as I usually find myself doing. The truth, I think, is that he had the impact of the star before whom resistance melts away, a phenomenon quite beyond the normal procedures of moral accounting.

The mystery of the star performer can only leave the inquiring mind confused, resentful, or blank, something that, of course, has the greatest political importance. Many Republicans have blamed the press for the attention Bill Clinton continued to get even out of office. Again, what they don't understand is that what a star says, and even what he does, is incidental to people's interest in him. When the click of empathic association is made with a leader, logic has very little to do with it and virtue even less, at least up to a certain distant point. Obviously, this is not very encouraging news for rational people who hope to uplift society by reasoned argument. But then, not many of us rational folk are completely immune to the star's ability to rule.

The presidency, in acting terms, is a heroic role. It is not one for comedians, sleek lover types, or second bananas. In a word, to be credible the man who acts as president must hold in himself an element of potential dangerousness. Something similar is required in a real star.

Like most people, I had never even heard of Marlon Brando the first time I saw him onstage not long after the end of World War II. The play was *Truckline Cafe*, a failed work by Maxwell Anderson that was soon to close, hardly a promising debut for an ambitious actor. The set is a shabby café on some country highway. In the version I saw (somewhat dif-

ferent than the published one), the place is empty
and miserably lit and it is after midnight. There are a
counter and a few booths with worn upholstery.
Now a car is heard stopping outside. Presently a
young man wearing a worn leather jacket and a cap
strolls in, an exhausted-looking girl behind him. He
saunters down to center stage, looking around for a
sign of life. For a long time he says absolutely nothing, just stands there in the sort of slouch you fall
into after driving for hours. The moment lengthens
as he tries to figure what to do, his patience clearly
thinning. Nothing has happened, he has hardly even
moved, but watching him, the audience, myself
included, is already spellbound. Another actor would
simply have aroused impatience, but we are in
Brando's power; we read him; his inner being is
speaking to us even if we can't make out precisely
what it is saying. Like an animal that has slipped
from its cage, the fellow is packed with all kinds of

The actor as actor

possibilities. Is he dangerous? Friendly? Stupid? Intelligent? Without a word spoken, this actor has opened up in the audience a whole range of emotional possibilities, including, oddly enough, a little fear. Finally he calls out, "Anybody here?!" What a relief! He has not shot up the place. He has not thrown chairs around. All he wanted, apparently, was a sandwich.

I can't explain how Brando, without a word spoken, did what he did, but he had found a way, no doubt instinctively, to master a paradox—he had implicitly threatened us and then given us pardon. Here was Napoleon, here was Caesar, here was Roosevelt. Brando had not asked the members of the audience to merely love him; that is only charm. He had made them wish that he would deign to love *them*. That is a star. Onstage or off, that is power, no different in its essence than the power that can lead nations.

And of course onstage or in the White House,

power changes everything, even including how the aspirant looks after he wins. I remember running into Dustin Hoffman on a rainy New York street some years ago; he had only a month earlier played the part of the Lomans' pale and nervous next-door neighbor Bernard in a recording session with Lee Cobb of *Death of a Salesman.* Now as he approached, counting the cracks in the sidewalk, hatless, his wet hair dripping, a worn coat collar turned up, I prepared to greet him, thinking that with his bad skin, hawkish nose and adenoidal voice some brave friend really ought to tell him to go into another line of work. As compassionately as possible I asked what he was doing now, and with a rather apologetic sigh he said, after several sniffles, "Well, they want me for a movie." "Oh?" I felt relieved that he was not to collapse in front of me in a fit of depression. "What's the movie?"

"It's called *The Graduate,*" he said.

"Good part?"

"Well, yeah, I guess it's the lead."

In no time at all this half-drowned puppy would have millions of people at his feet all over the world. And once having ascended to power, so to speak, it became hard even for me to remember him when he was real. Not that he wasn't real, just that he was real plus. And the plus is the mystery of the patina, the glow that power paints on the human being.

The amount of acting required of both President Bush and the Democrats is awesome now, given the fractured election and donation by the Supreme Court. Practically no participant in the whole process can really say out loud what is in his heart. They are all facing an ice-cold shower with a gun to their head. Bush has to act as though he were elected, the Supreme Court has to act as though it were the Supreme Court, Gore has to act as though he were practically overjoyed at his own defeat, and so on. It is all very theatrical but the closest thing to a deliberately rehearsed passion that I witnessed was the organized mob of Republicans banging threateningly on the door of a Florida vote-counting office and howling for the officials inside to stop counting. Watching this outburst I could practically hear the rehearsal, which of course they did. I must confess, though, that as a playwright I would be flummoxed as to how to make plausible on the stage an organized stampede of partisans yelling to stop the count and in the same breath accusing the other side of trying to steal the election. I can't imagine an audience taking this for anything but a satirical farce. But it was reality, the political kind, which easily spills over into the sort of chaotic dream where a cockroach becomes a Cadillac, which in turn turns into the Grand Canyon.

An election, not unlike a classic play, has a certain strict form that requires us to pass through certain

How a chad fell

ordained steps to a logical conclusion. When, instead, the form dissolves and chaos reigns, what is left behind—no differently than in the theater—is a sense in the audience of having been cheated and even mocked. After this last, most hallucinatory of elections, it was said that in the end the system worked, when clearly it hadn't at all. And one of the signs that it had collapsed popped up even before the decision was finally made in Bush's favor; it was when Dick Armey, the Republican majority leader in the House of Representatives, declared that he would simply not attend the inauguration if Gore was elected, despite immemorial custom and his obligation to do so as a leader of the Congress. In short, Armey had reached the limits of his actor's imagination and could only collapse into playing himself. But in the middle of a play you cannot have a major performer deciding to leave the scene without utterly destroying the whole illusion. For the system to be said to have worked, no one is allowed to stop acting.

The notable absence of any great affection or love for the candidates also suggests some distinct correlations in the theater. The play without a character we can really root for is in trouble. Shakespeare's *Coriolanus* is an example. It is not often produced, powerful though it is as playwriting and poetry, no doubt because, as a totally honest picture of ambition in a frightening human being, the closest he ever gets to love is Coriolanus' subservience to his mother. In short, it is a truthful play without sentimentality, and truthfulness, I'm afraid, doesn't sell a whole lot of tickets or draw votes. Which inevitably brings me again to Clinton. Until the revulsion brought on by the pardon scandal, he was leaving office with the highest rating for performance and the lowest for personal character. Translated—people had prospered under his leadership, and, with whatever

*". . . if I went into politics I could stay acting
and never change roles."*

reluctance, they still connected with his humanity as they glimpsed it, ironically enough, through his sins. We are back, I think, to the mystery of the star. Clinton, except for those few minutes when lying about Monica Lewinsky, was relaxed on camera in a way any actor would envy. And relaxation is the soul of the art, for one thing because it arouses receptivity rather than defensiveness in an audience.

That receptivity brings to mind a friend of mine who, many years ago, won the prize for selling more Electrolux vacuum cleaners in the Bronx than any other door-to-door salesman. He once explained how he did it. "You want them to start saying yes. So you ask questions that they can't say no to. Is this 1350 Jerome Avenue? Yes. Is your name Smith? Yes. Do you have carpets? Yes. A vaccuum cleaner? Yes. Once you've got them on a yes roll, a kind of psychological fusion takes place. You're both on the same side. It's almost like some kind of love, and they feel it's impolite for them to say no, and in no time you're in the house unpacking the machine." What Clinton projects is a personal interest in the customer that comes across as a sort of love. There can be no doubt that, like all great performers, he loves to act, he is most alive when he's on. His love of acting may be his most authentic emotion, the realest thing about him, and, as with Reagan, there is no dividing line between his performance and himself—he is his performance. There is no greater contrast than with Gore or Bush, both of whom projected a kind of embarrassment at having to perform, an underlying tension between themselves and the role, and tension, needless to say, shuts down love on the platform no less than it does in bed.

On every side there is a certain amount of lamenting about the reluctance of Americans to utterly condemn Bill Clinton, but rather than blaming their failed moral judgment I think we would do better to examine his acting. Clinton, to me, is our Eulenspiegel, the mythical arch prankster of fourteenth-century Germany who was a sort of mischievous and lovable folk spirit, half child, half man. Eulenspiegel challenged society with his enviable guile and a charm so irresistible that he could blurt out embarrassing truths about the powerful now and then, earning the gratitude of the ordinary man. His closest American equivalent is Brer Rabbit, who ravishes people's vegetable gardens and, just when he seems to be cornered, charmingly distracts his pursuer with some outrageously engaging story, long enough to let him edge closer and closer to a hole down which he escapes. Appropriately enough, the word *Eulenspiegel* is a sort of German joke: it means a mirror put before an owl, and since an owl is blind in daylight it cannot see its own reflection. So as bright and happy and hilariously unpredictable as Eulenspiegel is, he cannot see himself, and so, among other things, he is dangerous. In other words, a star. Indeed, the most perfect model of both star and political leader is that smiling and implicitly dangerous man who likes you.

In part, I think, it was because neither Gore nor Bush was particularly threatening that their offer of protective affection was not considered very important. Gore was so busy trying to unbend that he forfeited whatever menace he may have had, and while Bush did his best to pump up his chest and toughly turn down the corners of his mouth to show he was no pushover, it was all too obviously a performance, and for too long his opponents failed to take him as anything more than the potential president of a fraternity. In any case, he so understood what people needed to hear that a number of times, risking immodesty, to say the least, he actually referred to himself as a "leader" and claimed that his forthcoming administration would fill the vacuum of "leader-

Till Eulenspiegel

ship." Caught time after time fouling up his syntax, thus shaking the image of manly command, he has improved since the sparkling magic veil of real power has descended upon him, and his sentences, saving on grammar, have gotten shorter and shorter—to the point where, at times, he comes close to sounding like a gunslinger in a Clint Eastwood film. But he is beginning to relax into his role and, like most presidents, may in the fullness of time come to seem inevitable.

The ultimate foundation of political power, of course, has never changed: it is the leader's willingness to resort to violence should the need arise. But even this is too simple; Adlai Stevenson may have seemed too civilized to resort to violence without a crippling hesitation, and Jimmy Carter was so clearly restrained by Christian scruple that a single military accident involving a handful of unfortunate soldiers in one stroke destroyed all his credibility. An

American leader may deliver the Sunday lesson provided his sword is never out of reach, the two best examples being FDR and John Kennedy. But this type, which doesn't come along every day, is the aristocratic populist and the aristocrat learns how to act at a very early age; acting is part of his upbringing. A Nixon, on the contrary, has to learn as he goes along. Indeed, once he had ordered himself bugged, Nixon was literally acting during all his waking hours; his entire working life became a recorded performance.

The case of President Truman and the atom bomb is particularly rich in its references to acting and power. When several of the scientists who had built the first bomb petitioned Truman to stage a demonstration off the Japanese coast rather than dropping it on an inhabited city, he chose the latter course; the fear was that the first bomb might fail to work, encouraging the Japanese to even more resolutely refuse peace overtures, thus intensifying the war. However frightful its consequences, it was better, so it was claimed, to bomb a city and in one flash bring the war to an end. The weakness in this reasoning is that if the bomb was in fact so uncertain to explode, why drop it on a city, where Japanese scientists might examine and maybe even copy it?

A more persuasive argument, I'm afraid, is that if the bomb had been dropped in the ocean after the Japanese had been warned to expect a demonstration of a terrible new weapon, and it had been a dud, a dead iron ball splashing into the sea, Truman's unwillingness to kill would have threatened his leadership altogether, and his power, personally and symbolically, would have lost credibility. I'm not at all sure even now what I would have done in his position, confronted with the possibility of terrible American losses in a land invasion of Japan. But the issue is not Truman so much as the manifestations of power that people require their leaders to personify and act out.

Jesus Christ could not have beaten Hitler's Germany or Imperial Japan into surrender. And it is not impossible that our main reason for cloaking our leaders with a certain magical, extra-human, theatrical aura is to help disguise one of the basic conditions of their employment—namely, a readiness to kill for us. One need only scan the list of what are normally called the "great presidents" to realize that they were all leaders in war. Washington, Jackson, Lincoln, Theodore Roosevelt, Wilson, Franklin Roosevelt, Truman—to be sure war was not all they did but without it a dimension of their dominance would never have shown itself; it is the dimension of that solemnity which only a surrounding of death can lend to our imaginations. As war leader, a president rises to the stature of tragic figure touched by the arcane, the superhuman, entrusted as he is with not only the lives of our sons and daughters but the purity of the ideals which justify their sacrifice. It may well be that the great sea change in American politics, which is generally recognized as the gift of the sixties, was really brought to pass by Lyndon Johnson's retreat from the challenge of running for another term, given America's failure to subdue the Vietnamese Communists. Despite his great accomplishments in civil rights, education and other fields, he could no longer keep Americans from turning against the war and himself; in theatrical terms, he had stepped out of the story and his role in it to reveal himself as merely a tired, rejected, old man. Events had stripped him of his star's credibility, the power to dominate the stage, and he had devolved into a rather ordinary player smaller than his costume, his rank and his elevated throne merely emphasizing his failed ordinariness. In other words, his failure in Vietnam had stripped him of the dangerousness of the star-leader.

In a democracy, given the need for compromise

in every direction, the shortest distance between two points is often a crooked line, and so it is sadly inevitable that maintaining leadership requires the artifices of theatrical illusion. While Roosevelt was stoutly repeating his determination to keep America out of any foreign war, he was taking steps toward belligerency in order to save England and prevent a Nazi victory. In effect, mankind is in debt to his lies. So from the tragic necessity of dissimulation there seems to be no escape. Except, of course, to tell people the truth, something that doesn't require acting but may damage one's own party and, indeed, in certain circumstances, the human enterprise itself. Then what?

Then, I'm afraid, we can only turn to the release of art, to the other theater, the theater-theater where you can tell the truth without killing anybody and may even illuminate the awesomely durable dilemma of how to lead without lying too much. The release of art will not forge a cannon or pave a street, but it may remind us again and again of the corruptive essence of power, its immemorial tendency to enhance itself at the expense of humanity. The director and critic the late Harold Clurman called theater "lies like truth." Theater does indeed lie, fabricating everything from the storm's roar to the fake lark's song, from the actor's calculated laughter to his nightly flood of tears. And the actor lies; but with all the spontaneity that careful calculation can lend him, he may nevertheless construct a vision of some important truth about the human condition that opens us to a new understanding of ourselves. In the end, we call a work of art trivial when it illuminates little beyond its own devices, and the same goes for political leaders who bespeak some narrow interest rather than those of the national or universal good. The fault is not in the use of the theatrical arts but in their purpose.

Paradox is the name of the game where acting as

an art is concerned. It is a rare, hardheaded politician who is at home with any of the arts these days. To most political people the artist is a strange bird, somehow suspect, a nuisance, a threat to morality, or a fraud. At the same time, the fourth most lucrative American export, not far behind airplanes, is art—namely, music and films.

But art has always been the revenge of the human spirit upon the shortsighted. Consider the sublime achievements of Greece and her military victories and defeats, the necrophilic grandeur of the Egyptians, the glory of the Romans, the awesome power of the Assyrians, the rise and fall of the Jews and their incomprehensible survival, and what are we left with but a handful of plays, essays, carved stones, and some strokes of paint on paper or the rock cave wall—in a word, art? The ironies abound. Artists are not particularly famous for their conformity with majority mores, but whatever is not turned into art disappears forever. It is very strange when you think about it, except for one thing that is not strange but quite logical: however dull or morally delinquent an artist may be, in his moment of creation, when his work pierces to the truth, he cannot dissimulate, he cannot fake it. Tolstoy once remarked that what we look for in a work of art is the revelation of the artist's soul, a glimpse of God. You can't act that.

Arthur Miller was born in New York City in 1915 and studied at the University of Michigan. His plays include *All My Sons* (1947), *Death of a Salesman* (1949), *The Crucible* (1953), *A View from the Bridge* and *A Memory of Two Mondays* (1955), *After the Fall* (1964), *Incident at Vichy* (1965), *The Price* (1968), *The Creation of the World and Other Business* (1972), and *The American Clock* (1980). He has also written two novels, *Focus* (1945) and *The Misfits,* which was filmed in 1960, and the text for *In Russia* (1969), *In the Country* (1977), and *Chinese Encounters* (1979), three books of photographs by Inge Morath. His most recent works include a memoir, *Timebends* (1987), the plays *The Ride Down Mt. Morgan* (1991), *The Last Yankee* (1993), *Broken Glass* (1994), and *Mr. Peters' Connections* (1999), and a collection of essays, *Echoes Down the Corridor: Collected Essays, 1944–2000* (2000). He has twice won the New York Drama Critics Circle Award, and in 1949 he was awarded the Pulitzer Prize.